Little People, BIG DREAMS™

ALEXANDER VON HUMBOLDT

Written by
Maria Isabel Sánchez Vegara

Illustrated by
Sally Agar

Frances Lincoln
Children's Books

In the Kingdom of Prussia lived a wealthy boy called Alexander. From a very young age, he was curious about everything to do with nature, from the bright stars in the sky to the tiny fireflies glowing in the garden.

His father was chamberlain of the royal household, but he died when Alexander was only ten. Hoping her children would also become loyal servants of the kingdom, his mother hired the best tutors to educate him and his older brother.

But Alexander had other plans! He dreamt of being a
scientific explorer. So after learning all about plants, rocks,
and animals in college and studying them all over Europe,
he crossed the ocean eager to see the rest of the world.

In 1799, Alexander and his friend Aimé arrived in South America. He had not been on the continent for long when he noticed that the beautiful lake of Valencia was drying up because European settlers were felling a forest nearby.

He was the first Western scientist to understand something Indigenous people had long known: trees store water, protect the soil, cool the air, and are home to many animals. By cutting down trees, humans were harming the whole ecosystem.

Guided by Indigenous people, Alexander went up the Orinoco River into rain forests where no other Western scientist had ever been before. He drew maps and took notes on everything he found, even an electric eel whose shock could kill a person!

For months, he sketched and measured the Andes mountains and their nearby volcanoes, sometimes putting his life in danger. One day, an earthquake hit. Instead of panicking, he calmly set out his instruments to time it.

Alexander climbed Chimborazo, the highest known mountain at the time by Western travelers. Looking down at the landscape before him, he realized that clouds, mountains, rivers, meadows, and jungles were all connected. The Earth was one living being!

With the help of Indigenous guides and the most sophisticated instruments of his time, he crossed Mexico from coast to coast and measured everything. He was the first to draw maps showing the air temperature, a technique still used in weather forecasts.

Alexander learned of so many things that hundreds of rivers, mountains, plants, and animals were named after him.

Humboldt River

Orinoco River Dolphin
Inia geoffrensis humboldtiana

Humboldt's Squirrel Monkey
Saimiri cassiquiarensis

Humboldt Falls

Humboldt Penguin
Spheniscus humboldti

Humboldt Current

There was a glacier, a waterfall, a hog-nosed skunk…
Even a giant Humboldt Squid swam in the Humboldt Current!

Humboldt Glacier

Humboldt's Hog-nosed Skunk
Conepatus humboldtii

Russula humboldtii

ammillaria humboldtii

Humboldt's Lily
Lilium humboldtii

Humboldt Squid
Dosidicus gigas

Back in Europe, Alexander was thought of as a hero. Still, his biggest task was about to start: organizing everything he had collected and putting his findings on paper. He hoped it would take him two years, but it kept him busy for more than twenty.

Alexander was 76 when he published his most famous work, *Kosmos*. It was a fantastic journey across all of creation, from distant galaxies to oceans, volcanoes, mountains, plants, rocks, and tiny creatures.

By being the first Western scientist to describe the unity of nature, little Alexander changed the way that many people see our world.

Because we all live on a planet full of wonders where everything is connected.

ALEXANDER VON HUMBOLDT

(Born 1769 – Died 1859)

c. 1806

1814

Friedrich Wilhelm Heinrich Alexander von Humboldt was born on September 14th 1769 in Berlin, Prussia (modern-day Germany). After the death of their father, Alexander and his brother Wilhelm were raised by their mother who had the boys privately educated to allow them to qualify for high-ranking jobs in public office. As a kid, Alexander collected plants and shells. As an adult, he spent time studying economics in college, but became interested in geology and soon realized that his childhood hobby of nature was his true passion in life. Deciding to embark on a daring expedition, from 1799 he spent five years in Central and South America along with French botanist Aimé Bonpland. Guided by local Indigenous people, they climbed volcanoes and journeyed through lush rain forests, recording everything they found

1843

1850

along the way. Alexander's ascent of Ecuador's Chimborazo, without the help of modern mountaineering equipment, remained a mountain-climbing record from a Western perspective for nearly 30 years. Along his travels, he learned that Earth was one large ecosystem and he brought this information back to Western society upon his return to Europe. He spent the rest of his life cataloging his findings and writing books, including *Kosmos*, one of the most ambitious scientific works ever published. Hundreds of animals, plants, rivers, and mountains were named after him, although many of these things had and still have names in Indigenous languages. Alexander is remembered as the first Western scientist to recognize the importance and unity of nature across the world.

Want to find out more about **Alexander von Humboldt?**

Have a read of this great book:

The Incredible Yet True Adventures of Alexander von Humboldt
by Volker Mehnert

Brimming with creative inspiration, how-to projects, and useful information to enrich your everyday life, quarto.com is a favorite destination for those pursuing their interests and passions.

Text © 2022 Maria Isabel Sánchez Vegara. Illustrations © 2022 Sally Agar.

Little People Big Dreams and Pequeña&Grande are registered trademarks of Alba Editorial, SLU for books, publications and e-books. Produced under licence from Alba Editorial, SLU.

First Published in the USA in 2022 by Frances Lincoln Children's Books, an imprint of The Quarto Group.

Quarto Boston North Shore, 100 Cummings Center, Suite 265D, Beverly, MA 01915, USA

Tel: +1 978-282-9590, Fax: +1 978-283-2742 **www.Quarto.com**

A catalogue record for this book is available from the British Library.

ISBN 978-0-7112-7124-1

Set in Futura BT.

Published by Peter Marley • Designed by Lyli Feng

Edited by Lucy Menzies and Claire Saunders • Production by Nikki Ingram

Editorial Assistance from Rachel Robinson

Manufactured in Guangdong, China CC032022

1 3 5 7 9 8 6 4 2

Photographic acknowledgements (pages 28-29, from left to right): 1. Alexander von Humboldt by Friedrich Georg Weitsch, 1806 © GL Archive via Alamy Images. 2. ALEXANDER von HUMBOLDT (1769-1859) Prussian naturalist, explorer and scientist in a self portrait dated 1814 © Pictorial Press Ltd via Alamy Images. 3. Alexander von Humboldt, 1843 by Joseph Karl Stieler © GL Archive via Alamy Images. 4. Portrait, from a painting, of German naturalist and explorer, Alexander von Humboldt (1769-1859), circa 1850. © Paul Popper/ Popperfoto via Getty Images

Collect the Little People, **BIG DREAMS**™ series:

FRIDA KAHLO	**COCO CHANEL**	**MAYA ANGELOU**	**AMELIA EARHART**	**AGATHA CHRISTIE**	**MARIE CURIE**	**ROSA PARKS**	**AUDREY HEPBURN**

EMMELINE PANKHURST	**ELLA FITZGERALD**	**ADA LOVELACE**	**JANE AUSTEN**	**GEORGIA O'KEEFFE**	**HARRIET TUBMAN**	**ANNE FRANK**	**MOTHER TERESA**

 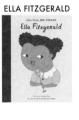      

JOSEPHINE BAKER	**L. M. MONTGOMERY**	**JANE GOODALL**	**SIMONE DE BEAUVOIR**	**MUHAMMAD ALI**	**STEPHEN HAWKING**	**MARIA MONTESSORI**	**VIVIENNE WESTWOOD**

MAHATMA GANDHI	**DAVID BOWIE**	**WILMA RUDOLPH**	**DOLLY PARTON**	**BRUCE LEE**	**RUDOLF NUREYEV**	**ZAHA HADID**	**MARY SHELLEY**

MARTIN LUTHER KING JR.	**DAVID ATTENBOROUGH**	**ASTRID LINDGREN**	**EVONNE GOOLAGONG**	**BOB DYLAN**	**ALAN TURING**	**BILLIE JEAN KING**	**GRETA THUNBERG**

JESSE OWENS	**JEAN-MICHEL BASQUIAT**	**ARETHA FRANKLIN**	**CORAZON AQUINO**	**PELÉ**	**ERNEST SHACKLETON**	**STEVE JOBS**	**AYRTON SENNA**

LOUISE BOURGEOIS	**ELTON JOHN**	**JOHN LENNON**	**PRINCE**	**CHARLES DARWIN**	**CAPTAIN TOM MOORE**	**HANS CHRISTIAN ANDERSEN**	**STEVIE WONDER**

MEGAN RAPINOE

MARY ANNING

MALALA YOUSAFZAI

ANDY WARHOL

RUPAUL

MICHELLE OBAMA

MINDY KALING

IRIS APFEL

ROSALIND FRANKLIN

RUTH BADER GINSBURG

MARILYN MONROE

KAMALA HARRIS

ALBERT EINSTEIN

CHARLES DICKENS

YOKO ONO
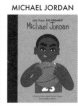

MICHAEL JORDAN

ROSALIND FRANKLIN

NELSON MANDELA

PABLO PICASSO

AMANDA GORMAN

GLORIA STEINEM

FLORENCE
NIGHTINGALE

HARRY HOUDINI

J.R.R. TOLKIEN

ELVIS PRESLEY

NEIL ARMSTRONG

ALEXANDER VON
HUMBOLDT

ACTIVITY BOOKS

STICKER ACTIVITY
BOOK

COLORING
BOOK

LITTLE ME, BIG
DREAMS JOURNAL

Discover more about the series at www.littlepeoplebigdreams.com